BROKEN WING

by

KJ GoForth

Gotham Books

30 N Gould St.
Ste. 20820, Sheridan, WY 82801
https://gothambooksinc.com/

Phone: 1 (307) 464-7800

© 2024 *KJ GoForth*. All rights reserved.

No part of this book may be reproduced, stored in a retrieval system, or transmitted by any means without the written permission of the author.

Published by Gotham Books (May 17, 2024)

ISBN: 979-8-88775-978-4 (H)
ISBN: 979-8-88775-976-0 (P)
ISBN: 979-8-88775-977-7 (E)

Because of the dynamic nature of the Internet, any web addresses or links contained in this book may have changed since publication and may no longer be valid.

The views expressed in this work are solely those of the author and do not necessarily reflect the views of the publisher, and the publisher hereby disclaims any responsibility for them.

INTRODUCTION

For any and all suffering souls buried in the strict dogma of Ideologies manipulation, this mind bending creative touch may help you to unlock our truest higher self giving you a look into what inspiration is about.

Torn from the tree for anew
Graft Rediscovering how to laugh

Adults and their issues children who scream
Don't understand the American dream

Fought for a country who doesn't care
Inside the wounds that we bare

Altar of alters kingdom of kings
Bored by possessions and other things

Back to the bunker chilling and cold
With a soul that has been sold

Indignant warlike banking on crime
Spreading narratives at dinner time

Locked and loaded looking to fight
Piling up bodies all through the night

Bring to me my dove in white
Join our hearts in sheer delight

Be the guidance show your grace
Give life meaning in this place

Keep us safe from illusions scams
Be the pearl of these hands

Read what's written on hearts of gold
The ones of yours that can't be sold

Dance with pleasure sing it loud
Help us standout in any crowd

Embrace our goals see them through
And never forget I'm here for you

Patchworks painting realities form
Each an aspect to conform

Same not really nothing seems right
Out of this life we must take a big bite

Sour apples sour grapes
Ferment into something great

Dulling the senses capturing crud
In dirty water under the mud

Mystic beginning cosmic end
A DNA with a special blend

Shoot the messenger I don't care
Between these legs is a large pair

A child in need from the vine of a tree
One with the wisdom to be happy and free

Striving to see through the curtains veil
Not understanding her own spiritual jail

Separations witness fighting it's fight
Piercing the heart of her inner light

Born to inspire and have a good dream
After cleaning the dirt on her screen

Conscious decisions with follow through
To enter the mystery of life's greatest stew

Plenty of power and beautiful grace
With something inside without replace

At the water's edge of reality and dreams
Lives sound voices and the screams

A watery grave of the dreamers realm
Surrendered to source hands off the helm

Reaching for illusions passing up bait
Passing through time at a different rate

Sideways sometimes to collect
Pathways in life without respect

Butchered lifetimes caught in the clinch
Energy tied to a traditional grinch

Glory to the age of golden truth
When what's revealed will come with proof

At a distance we watch an arm's length away
Healing prospectives in a new way

Providing the insight to carry the pure
Because love was always the cure

More than a word or attitude
An intuition that does conclude

A precious position to perceive
No matter WTF you believe

The garden gates to our inner place
If the scars have no trace

*Unwavering trust in the eye of the storm
Making a pitch so we can transform*

*Wheats been ground flowers prepped
How many secrets have you kept*

*Confidential classified redacted words
Information warfare controlling the herds*

*Black book diary blackmails codes
As the soul of a nation slowly erodes*

*Lock-N-Step left or right
Leveraging the power in a proxy fight*

*Damned if we do
Damned if we don't*

Refreshing breath of a soul alive
On a timeline above the hive

Built to harbor unlimited light
With the fuel to sustain one long flight

Chip off the block shoulders strong
In alignment with her hearts song

Graced to glow happy to sing
Alert and aware of everything

Magic of her heart piercing through
The clouds of darkness she use to knew

Army of angels at her beckoning call
Firmly committed to standing tall

Dogmatism and it's dirty hands
Can not replace a love that spans

Throughout each walking day on earth
As we create and give birth

To inspire works of art
Trusting each will be a part

For the greater good of wisdoms guide
So the truly gifted don't need to hide

Amongst the shadows of authority lines
Burying us deep within the vines

Confident with much to give
With this life we love to live

Just a moment wait and see
Those once dead eyes now have glee

You may not know what it's like
When the target of love is a strike

Showered in tranquil golden vibe
When two whole souls do collide

A mirrored reflection in a blissful state
When compromise is not the bait

The best and worst healed for good
With light maintenance we've understood

Without the illusion of deaths dark door
We become whole at our core

I pledge no allegiance to any flag
On any continent for no bag

There is no republic to which deserves
The kind of respect it hasn't preserved

Never a nation built on greed
Will have the ability to grow good seed

Behind the clown show goons rejoice
Silencing freedom cutting off choice

Collection of lies limiting growth
Material accomplishments it always does boast

Pectoral of dreams hiding our truths
Under the big top we find plenty of goofs

A hardened heart full of stones
With a stubborn face filled with frowns

Nothing ever good enough
Not enough storage to put your stuff

Purposely plotting distractions in place
Silently moving but leaving a trace

Territory marked like a pissing dog
Collapsing the trap to capture the hog

Eat from the trough and get sick
Chose a poison that will get you quick

Landscape of tears and sorrows friends
Get what you give as energy sends

*Show the presence make me trust
That this life is more than lust*

*Back that butt up to the fire
Summon the angles of your choir*

*Lift this reality erase it's wrongs
Inspire the lifted to sing new songs*

*Be the bearer of new fruit
Help us give conformity one big boot*

*Yours to mold us receive
Close the eyes of he who deceives*

*Portion out courage give us strength
Let peace fill hearts as we rise in rank*

Open access to he who dares
To bring back that which is shared

A melody of my stories vivid and warm
The sort of message that doesn't do harm

Dedication on firm ground
Through the distractions making sounds

Millions of miles millions of turns
Sometimes somethings make hearts burn

Through each fire around each bend
Surely somewhere we no longer pretend

Sturing to mix and incorporate
What freedom is before it's too late

Dangerous dreams to free the mind
Inspired to leave conformity behind

Ruled by conscious free will
Not commanded what to do

Choosing reality that fits a vibe
Won't be strung out on any false ride

Malice mayhem not a friend
Proxy dogma killing itself to the end

Embroiled in carnage of it's doing
As a people we should start suing

Mental anguish emotional jail
Yes I sense a large betrayal

Our own hope our own ray
Put there for that rainy day

No one's credit but our own
When we wake and are shown

What exists at our core
And the connection we have all bore

Back to basics wants on hold
Like material things lust of gold

Love trust honor respect
Without it we only write a blank check

In our hearts on our backs
We stand strong and divert attacks

Moved by love memories guide
What it was to be inside

Birthed to be born to bring
Out the best of everything

Duality doomed but a needed move
So gratefulness could find it's grove

Clarity beaming hostage set free
Eyes are not the only way to see

Closet of skulls set ablaze
When heart and mind are free of haze

Womb of creation gift of all gifts
Spirit on high as love lifts

Scripture sculpting tyrannies twist
Bound to babel lies persist

Collection of papers in dead men's vaults
Pointing fingers with blame and faults

Preponderance of evidence in it's acts
Banking on power with it's ax

Ripe with stench smelling foul
To much ego to throw in the towel

Preying outside through one man's blood
Worshiping madness and all of that crud

Cult like cradle of what lifes about
With black floors and blood as grout

Hijacked head heart space scared
Dimming the light from cosmic stars

Each a temple each of source
Through these veins truth does course

Fields tilled planted crop
The lunatics will never stop

Passed with rules led by fools
Profiting endless through It's schools

Patterns of thought that conformity bought
Salvation seekers are always sought

Humming Hive of the hornets nest
Maybe your power should take a rest

Resistance futile when you get got
When we step up and take our shot

Backward impossible landmines laid
Facing forward focus stayed

Shifting to see grown to grow
With anticipation of some great show

Stop signs removed green lights galore
Thankful we're not alone in this score

Too many times to proud to quite
This time feels a good fit

Circular motion back to the start
The beginning and end of each heart

*One at a time the world sees change
When we question what authority claims*

*With healthy view of what tastes foul
How narratives remove us from the now*

*Serious claims of adultism blames
Varying sames after the flames*

*Free to speak free to feel
Laying claim we need to heal*

*Past transgressions of oppressions
One at a time powers successions*

*Number sequences astral aim
Change the order and win the game*

That which was laid at your feet
Has a memory and a beat

It's been there since the day we met
Not my fault wasn't the bet

Don't fully understand how this could be
But what I give I share for free

You summoned me not me you
Was your intention for one to be two

There's no replacement for who you are
There is a bond that is felt from afar

Corny maybe crazy for sure
How could a love be so pure

*A bunch of people with a bunch of pain
Bringing down high vibe we gain*

*Toxic treason as to why we're here
Filled with anger shame and fear*

*Apparatus mode bound to history's fails
Spiritual enslavement emotional jails*

*Operation guilt swindled by the con
Another twisted cult like pawn*

*Dark and light do exist
But the story will have a strange twist*

*Reserve your ticket while you can
Defeat the illusion that has been ran*

No more gray skies or falling rain
After the healing from what was pain

Encrypted encoded deep within
A place where peace claims a win

An inner voice calling us home
Where love comes first in every bone

Slowed to face the rise and shine
So our truths can guide the blind

Partaking in mysteries and life's greatest trials
Out the other side with laughs and smiles

Who could have known what awaits
When each truth become our own gates

To an unaware empty soul
With the missing part that was stole

Your chance is here in the now
If you try you'll find out how

With destiny calling to fill a role
Leaving behind what has taken a toll

Free will favored control cut loose
Along with narratives that formed a noose

Why delay are you scared
Life is nothing but dare

With one brain cell and heart of gold
Our greatest gifts have been sold

Created to collapse conformities guise
Digging deep exposing lies

Psychological emotional entrapments dean
Projecting authority over everything

Balance stacked on a lopsided scale
Hellen Keller read with braille

Itchy scars that once were scabs
Now are healed outside authorities blabs

A life of our own purely to learn
To reconnect in innocence and let our hearts burn

Volunteered at a risk keeping an oath
The time is now for humanities to grow

The further I go the more the cost
Leaving people who are still lost

Tried to reach out tried to explain
What happens spiritually when we live in pain

What was found was always there
Just needed a push to expose and bare

Excited and lite landing in tune
Shoveling shit with a large spoon

Trimming fat scraping skin
So the proper restart will win

Eased to rest sleeping well
Like we say time will tell

Just cuz you can doesn't mean you should
Sometimes stuff is misunderstood

Sometimes friends for whom we care
May slam a door laugh and stare

Stare at this with jealous envy
And ask yourself how can this be

Coat tale riders not allowed
I don't hang with that crowd

Stationary thought not a fan
Rationalism should have a ban

With my mystic merry band
Is where I'll make it as I stand

Whipped to a frenzy pill bottles explode
When we let power pave our road

Leeches and layers playing a part
As their illusion targets our heart

Adultism madness imposing its will
Chemical suicide in each pill

Correcting behavior in a toxic mix
Western medicine causing more sicks

Disconnect glaring writing more scripts
Needles of toxic giving us pricks

Chemical industry leading the way
To a cataclysm where we will pay

Holding dark lit by light
Mirroring an image that just might

Twisted tales or manly facts
Pre-clandestine anal attacks

Profiteering on honey and milk
Gems gold spices and silk

Obsessed disorders sinking the soul
Social media is our new troll

AI mix controlled by greed
Propagandas tool to feed dead seed

Keeping us hostage bonded and bound
Plugging our ears from positive sound

Quick to react slow to respond
An introduction from the beyond

Opportunity to heal to grow and become
Leaving behind a life of numb

Free from the traps of obligations request
Viewing this life as a treasure chest

Open and willing grateful and kind
When fractures align with what we find

Ascending the depths of sorrow and hurt
Generating love as to assert

Property pirates that scared this heart
The time has come for you to depart

Immensely moved to shock and awe
Trained in love so hearts can thaw

Caterpillar to butterfly
Metamorphic if we try

Sacral voice brought to life
When our free will has a choice

Generations of apples in our pie
Yet what was stolen still makes us cry

Without concept of nature's signs
Separation covers crimes

Acts of kindness don't compensate
When her fury affects each state

Fields of green under moon like skies
Spring has sprung in balance surprise

Nature's wonders supportive to health
A subtle reminder to what is wealth

To experience the whats and whys
To train our wings so that we may fly

An ancient wisdom that ignores time
And any a prophets that can't rhyme

Slippery sidewalks on downward slopes
2000 years of empty hopes

Not gonna take it not gonna bow
Laughing at authority having a cow

Ain't no describing what we've found
Ain't no laws that we are bound

One soul to another step by step
We hold the key to what's been kept

Induced by a union odds stacked against
Who could have known any future events

Starry eyes wishing for hope
That the candle we burn can teach us to cope

In an upside down world filled with peril
My love for you is in my marrow

Pressed to my core my anguish leaves
Like leafs of fall from the trees

In the fleeting thoughts as love walks blind
Along rough roads where no one's kind

Entrusted feelings that lead to peace
When the toxic has come to cease

Wronged to right to test trust
With a heart ready to bust

Inventory taken to reflect
No reputation to protect

Life goes on so it seems
New beginnings are worth more than beans

This cosmic dance between the veils
Must surely give back with full pales

Moon on the horizon under starry skies
Asking the universe for a prize

Life times wondering homeless and sick
Abandoned and lonely must be a trick

A reality a place where to begin
Where true love is not allowed to win

Practicing kindness to pay respect
With this conscience I write this check

Balanced and whole one of the one
Swapping stories having fun

Kinetic in nature magnetized
No negative will polarize

Too close for comfort to far to see
Keeping a promise living life free

Projected nonsense always at bay
Staying focused on the now of the day

Hydrated and healthy 3rd eye open
Being inspired by love not hoping

Meaning to mention words don't explain
Light and dark don't feel the same

Held to fire but didn't get burned
Did the work and the light was earned

Seeded by light soiled by dark
Time for a walk in a nice park

At the window of thought free to each mind
A path to our core so we are not blind

A healed heart a defragmented head
Intuition grown negative dead

Step by step day by day
I own me and thats my way

Two to one separation gone
Sandcastles built didn't make the dawn

Half to whole out of the trench
Not a poster child for any wench

Careful and kind loving and free
Planting new seed for a new tree

Eager and willing channeling source
Pleased by peace and tranquilities course

In secret I write invisible I glide
Brining back messages I no longer hide

Ghost writing with pen papers transformed
What once was blank now has forms

Blessed to be stoic in style
So many reasons to laugh and smile

Careful and caring as the mirror reflects
Seeing through what power protects

Penalty shootout last to go
The winning goal has stole the show

Seemingly senseless capturing steam
Vigilant and focused like a laser beam

Dropped expectations filling that void
Remembering only what's been enjoyed

Trusting intuitive head to gut
Door stays open never shut

Field of roses without thorns
Where negative has no horns

A weathered storm to find out
What this life can be about

Able to hold the light within
So there's no starting over again

Rendering results theories exposed
Rising above the many dead souls

Halfwit logic measured by power
What it sees it shall devour

Excuses blame justify
Desires burn while mothers cry

Side notes shifted supporting cause
All the while breaking laws

Artificial art of war
Peace has never been the core

Granted access to what I hold
This a soul that can't be sold

One sharp edge left to go
The one that pierced my heart and soul

Regretted acts carried with guilt
One last thing that must be spilt

My life has changed accept for you
It's our trust we must renew

Balanced with love unconditionally
Respecting each other with loyalty

This heart that throbs in this chest
Has eyes for you cuz you're the best

I know not normal so what's new
We could have what's made for two

What had to die to clear this path
Why what is near may have some rath

Sounds and symbols signs intense
New is coming to replace past tense

With healed heart and last brain cell
All that is all that shall

Protected always and thankful for
Grateful passing through each door

Lasting linger been dismissed
As if this grace has been kissed

Show us greatness lift our eyes
Expunge our secrets expose our lies

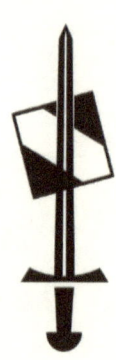

Still alone still alive
Disconnected from the hive

Forging forward forging past
As a castout of the cast

Free to find free to be
Getting over being lonely

Sprung to action sprung to great
With another level to activate

Learned to love learned to see
Learned this world is not for me

Passed each test passed my way
So what's the point in why I stay

In the name of compassion at our core
Like a young child in a candy store

Each with a favorite each with a path
Leading to new green fields of grass

Burdons lost obligations blown
With sights set on the unknown

Controls illusion no longer a thing
No longer this weight has a sting

Service to self service to source
Caring about individual course

A cause-and-effect paradigm shift
Whatever it takes to defeat the grift

Rest easy my dear for all shall pass
You are a true warrior with a strong cast

Supported and seen anchoring light
With a beautiful aura that's very bright

With an essence unmatched and smiling heart
There for the needy doing her part

Wise past her years here for the show
Enigmatic with a glow

Out of the dragnet that caused a stall
Synchronistically moving having a ball

Feeling in flow bathed in milk
Skin so soft like Persian silk

Inside a vision living a dream
Every day a birthday with cake and ice cream

So much to explore perspectives to see
Learning the meaning of calamity

Washed over with wisdom gutters cleared
Staying the path no matter the sneer

Goodness and giving caring and kind
Turning inside to find whats to find

Treasured memories not of this ride
When the clearing is done and atoms collide

Positive change with lessons to collect
When we spend time to stop and reflect

Opening doors through golden gates
Knowing surely fate awaits

Picking and choosing what aligns
In the daily life of grinds

Holding visions deep in this soul
Unconditional love continues to grow

Patchwork of people knitted so fine
Sovern in nature guilted devine

Haloed heartspace charging ahead
Healing scars that begin in the head

Quantum we leap with wing on our backs
Lifting humanity with what's in our packs

Feeling the suck of a soulless vibe
One where hopelessness hides inside

Choices to makes on what comes next
Care to let go cuz I can't protect

Ready to run but fighting back
Can't let low vibe get me off track

Thought I understood thought I knew
Thought there was special between me and you

The door stays open to reconnect
But this ain't working with respect

My beautiful queen the choice is yours
Our life together can't be bought in stores

Invalidation causing a rift
Through time and space as we drift

Never a notion but embedded by love
Two lonely souls in one glove

Lifes not always easy nor is it fair
But worth living when we share and dare

Stepping to a beat barefoot on this earth
Creativity calling inspired from birth

No more waiting in line for this ride
When what's in our hearts will provide

A calling of spirit to dance on the moon
When two hearts collide and consume

A wonderful pallet to start anew
As we harvest what we grew

Seeds of time carried within
Cosmic beginning cosmic end

Windswept fields waters rage
All is set on this stage

Sweet ripe apples a hanging fruit
The trumpet wanes under the flute

Soft melodies caress and warm
When the swarm bring no harm

Peaches and plums pudden pie
Fruits of nature in creations eye

Open door access to a comfort zone
Where peace and love are always shown

Upside down in this planet gone mad
Where the norm seems to be sad

Contractual concepts burdons grand
Barrowed commandments with
lines in the sand

Sticky substance in its traps
Needing followers to fill its gaps

Clueless but clever talking points
Cults of men as it anoints

Clear cut needed for the standing dead
And a new oven to bake new bread

So many miles under these feets
Most spent on dead end streets

Trying to transmute cruel hard knocks
In worn out shoes with no socks

Wishful thinking won't get it done
Not enough energy to stay on the run

Target mounted square on my back
And I won't give up to much to unpack

Cosmic arrangement carrying weight
Out of my mind in this state

Born to bring born to fight
In the dark and the light

Pure in passion taking a leap
As the mountain tops keep getting steep

Hard to handle what compassion does
What can surface with an alluring buzz

To high to stop can't turn around
Never knowing what will be found

Runway taxi to power full tilt
You'll need a new heart for what I've built

Risen from ashes ready to rise
In blinding light that consumes my eyes

Door to the soul through where we peer
A concept to me that seems quite clear

Triggering timelines connecting the dots
In the dark I'm taking my shots

Honored to serve thankful to be
Not a puppet of conformity

Whisked away to my own cloud
One that doesn't have a crowd

Deciphering what's and why's
With an effort that always tries

Doing my best to makes sense
Why certain paths leave hardcore dents

Stripping back to expose
Holding steady to my rose

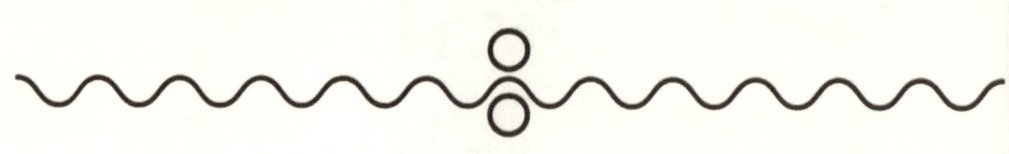

        Anew reality without chains
        Yes I know this sounds strange

    No presence of the boot on our neck
   No commandments will we have to check

    War and chaos and delusional ones
    Shall soon be taken it in the buns

  Answering the call addressing the scars
    Who will stand out among the stars

    Angst and anguish gone for good
    What was wrong has withstood

    Cleansing clearing bearing down
In the blink of an eye we'll hear no sound

Willful extermination of what didn't hatch
By a creed who lit the match

Expansionist confiscating what doesn't belong
Crushing spirit erasing song

Like a horror flick without ends
Justifying Jesus by killing friends

Happy enough to get ahead
No matter how much blood is shed

Believing one code is correct for all
Huddled together before the fall

Vigilant and ready for one man's return
Conformity never could discern

Toxic to test not run and hide
Only loyalty and trust do provide

When it gets tough the tough stand tall
Because in this game we own the ball

Stripped of dignity forced to slave
Killing neighbors was never brave

Justly cleansed to sterilize stock
From the pillar of a broken block

He who serves he who dies
She who's heart cries impression by lies

Back and forth battles chaos persist
When something that's served doesn't exist

A happy life is a healthy heart
Open to love no matter where we start

Epiphanies present in a moment moved
When emotions feel out of groove

Merging desires collapsing walls
No more echoes in empty halls

Exploring the unknown pleased to awake
Thinking to myself for goodness sake

Exuding the patience to support
Visions received from the highest court

Clickety-clack on a runaway train
Staying grounded to not go insane

Stop look and listen to create
Things that make us feel great

What we possess buried and cloaked
When we're not cut off and feeling choked

This plea goes out to avert
To end the pain and the hurt

To stop the lies and it's a support
And establish new laws in your court

To expose the corruption of ill fate
And expose the ones who exacerbate

Stop the war machine that murders and maims
Stop the evil from its killing games

Collapsing a kingdom to reset
Power waging war one sure bet

Greedy scumbags who posses the coin
And the secret societies that they join

To many of us so few of them
Robbing from each our true gem

Ticker tape parade coming for us
When the scum have no bus

Don't let illusions rob you blind
Stay within and you shall find

Followers following a worn out path
Because of tradition and fear of some wrath

Psychology ignorant dogma in words
Creating more and more hollow turds

Sick of salvation ruling the land
Promising something it calls grand

Spun out and spinning in its own way
Back to a corner where it will stay

Wiggle room in a white straight jacket
Gonna get ya if you can't hack it

Sick in humor yes I agree
Now I need to take a pee

Pleased to have passed through another space
Without leaving a negative trace

Conscious decisions free wills friend
Playing it cool right to the end

Signals beaming from my core
As I connect back to what I adore

A simple serving of love and peace
Boosting what we must increase

Redirected to regulate
Redefining what once was hate

Power to the people who stand as one
Did something happen to good old fun

With a light touch of love and a basket of joy
With an open heart is how to deploy

Filling the craters left by the hurt
And all the emotions covered in dirt

Skeletons exposed sterilized by tears
Perspectives change without fears

Knowledge and wisdom shall pre-cyst
Don't read the bible but i see the twist

Shackles of envy and pockets of greed
Are not what societies should need

Hefty doses of peace and love
Within this lifetime from above

Labeling the lost freeing the kind
Giving new vision to the blind

Identity crisis hijacking true self
Sick and bloated no concern for health

Clearly mistaken somethings gone wrong
Who created this planet we're on

Browbeaten innocence covering courage
One more tactic to discourage

Sick and tired of linear time
And the power drunk on wine

Low vibration vermin crawl
Who's proud enough to stand tall

If we don't open up we can't expand
And life will seem but a grain of sand

Legacy levers and creative crew
The time is now for me and you

Here to rejoice in what must change
We mustn't let authority keep us deranged

The forest can be thick and rivers deep
Sometimes the desert is good for a weep

We are the change we were born for this task
We have the strength when we take off our mask

Surrender to seek what's already ours
Here on this planet under the stars

Superficial mental break
Things we have what we take

Taken for granted in exchange
In a system that seems strange

Working for paper to support
Just to be taken in some court

Fighting for fairness against the rig
Who in this world is Mr. Big

Clarities focus must be out to lunch
And Mr. Big must be waiting for brunch

Clickity-clack this world is wack
Walking around with an axe in our back

Glad to have gossiped about your day
But on your side of the fence is where you'll stay

Filled out a form to conform
Cuz you need a job to stay safe from the mob

Congrats really the matrix owns you
It want's you to know that your through

Once in a lifetime maybe twice
Your waking essence will have a choice

Breakfree darling learn to fly
Leave the ground and say good-by

To patterns to ways to head games tricks
Give it a chance let's see what sticks

Watching a kingdom's wealth dry up
As it pours from an empty cup

Intimidation not working funeral fire burns
While the troops keep dying filling the yearns

What and why to fill a crave
Power digs another grave

Influence peddling loyalty lies
When corruption reins before our eyes

Insulated from the winter's snow
Waiting for the wind to blow

As writers write till the sun goes down
We know about each and every clown

Just slow down and breath deep
Give your tea time to steep

Relax to nothing but what we are
In a universe each a star

Roll in the grass take off your shoes
Whatever it takes to cure the blue's

Enjoy in nature what scenery lends
Reconnect to her love and become close friends

See with your heart hear with your eyes
Feel the sun and wind till the soul flies

Bring back the passion and play till we drop
There won't be a reason to call any cop

With the light of each day brings new hope
To paint a new picture and unravel each rope

As awakenings rise and we set ourselves free
We understand what we were meant to be

Our power our life to live and learn
My fire to ignite and let burn

False ego dead narcissists blocked
Don't care about what humans call clocks

Shift to awareness in each state
I must say it feels great

No more pretending what has become
Any and all of these lives into one

Amazing to mend what has brought hurt
In this world of slinging dirt

Holding a high vibe to resonate
Feeling the energy as to vibrate

Giving each moment what has been learnt
Holding some space for bridges that burnt

Respecting each breath it might be the last
Able to envision a future not past

The doorbell has rung the alarm bells have sound
To far we've come to loose sacred ground

Our heartbeats together we are as one
The trials we've been through haven't been fun

Mindfully moved through the fire
Being careful of any desire

What to me seems so real
What I've done to fully heal

A soul's journey out in the wild
One of a kind quite the child

Head water dreamer to harbor in trust
After the fall of greed and lust

Floating weightless between each scene
Never grew up love being a teen

Lasting lunacy your time has come
To histories memory you shall succumb

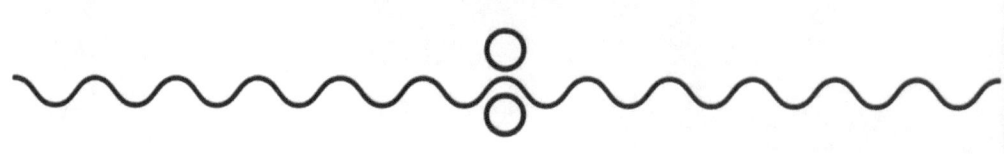

Waiting in line to help out a friend
Someone real not pretend

The miles we've traveled and the spaces seen
Together forever on the same team

Mustering courage on a trail unknown
Leaving a light on far from home

Instinctually guided looking for signs
Avoiding the chaos and it's crimes

A need to be inspired and to clear
Stay close to the heart that's near and dear

Hard knock lessons on a wide street
Holding a candle for everyone we meet

Alone in sleep alone all day
Something keeps pushing me away

Ready to run away from the past
To start over within a new cast

Wishing for wisdom standing firm
While what seemed real is a burn

Wandering warrior soul earned back
Found what was hiding under the stack

Set straight like an arrow but still a goof
Reality can change in one poof

Determined to stay on corrected course
Happy to know how to use the force

That one ounce of fear in your head
Is what has left your heart dead

Why in the world would this be
Through what sort of veil do thy see

Neurotic neurosis coupons clipped
Why can no one see what control has stripped

Carefully conditioned clutter installed
Compartmentalizing barely can crawl

Ignorance hiding behind symbolic signs
As righteous dicks hide their crimes

Pompous princess here's your rock
Time is sticking on one clock

Torn are the thoughts that stagnate growth
Going against the soul and its oath

Trapped are the vision that we hold
At our cores that have been sold

Gone is the wisdom exchanged for control
Life without meaning in a toilet bowl

Cesspool of head games claiming our hearts
Like a dagger separating parts

Reflection required gossip gone
Each our own truth from the dawn

A blinding future etched in gold
When we reclaim the soul we sold

I didn't know why I was born
Until I got lost in a field of corn

Wings were clipped sides were crushed
Always looking for the next rush

Suddenly night turned to day
Didn't understand the price I'd pay

Shutters slamming blaring horns
Mixed up movement bed of thorns

Gashes oozing poisonous lies
Exposing why most goodness dies

Bent on being best I can
From traumas past I have ran

Rockstar ready and in the groove
Over the bullshit with nothing to prove

Cage of rage taken a part
So this life could have a new start

Silent remembrance of all the trials
Of the organizations that reduced my miles

Wings to fly through tragedies traps
As my heart applauds and joyfully claps

Jurisdiction outer realm
With both hands at the helm

A comfort zone in a pleasing way
Some place I wish that I could stay

Keep unzipping compartments of crime
Like it's histories nursery rhyme

Justified action horrific acts
No wonder war winners rewrite facts

Sent to serve cleared to impale
What an empire does in its betrayal

Out of sync with orders to crush
Because killing gives it a rush

More and more never enough
Stealing other people stuff

Take your last breath feel the sward
He who controls the violent horde

*Pressed to pursue some other way
Conformity was never here to stay*

*A natural fit to split the core
On what's perceived to be the whore*

*Scary to think what ignorance has done
What it thinks is right and what it does shun*

*Inebriated from power in the killing fields
Counting dollars as it yields*

*Canary in the coal mine sounds the alarm
When what can't be seen will bring harm*

*Tare in the veil where I sneak back-n-forth
Adjusting my compass staying on course*

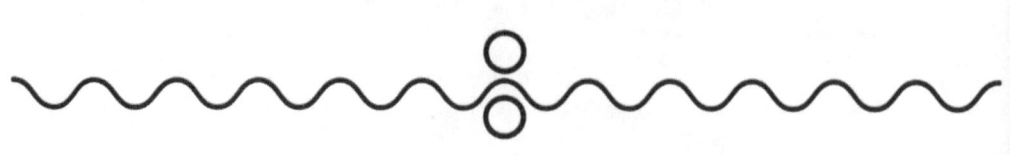

Picking ISM's that please my soul
Ignoring the one that take a toll

Glad for choices happy to change
Without limits wide in range

Ingenious ideologies with heavy hand
Only worth is in sand

Gold and glory conquest and greed
I must not understand what heathens need

Patriarchal power monarchy rule
Using war as it's tool

Instruments of ignorance laying claim
Doing business with its same

What I count is the scraps
I've had All put there to keep me mad

In the blink of an eye silhouettes change
Remembering why this life feels so strange

Gone are the emotions that impaired my sight
Gone are the blocks for me to write

Not one thing is worth more pain
On this planet that's gone insane

Finger on the pulse freedom's door
In amazement of what's in store

Fucking insane stuck in a box
Vaccinated for chickenpox

Not here to stand still in the shit
Won't be popped like that ugly zit

Sacrifice why to please some code
Here's my finger hit the road

Put up a barricade watch me move
No one can steal what I grove

Head game cowards living lies
Torching the earth burning the skies

Cloak waring scumbags feel my stare
Don't forget to ask if I care

Proceeding as planned instructions clear
Protecting what is held so dear

One of a kind never two
Singing sad songs to get through

In separation but never by heart
A love to strong to be torn apart

Glory to the people standing in love
It's the best of any drug

Perfectly balanced strangers unite
Embracing their truth snuggling all night

Pet names instead of porn
Bonded commitment that don't need sworn

Witness unneed traditions failed
Of a ship long since sailed

So far from home so many years
So much heartache so many fears

Separated at birth into this realm
Dropped here on earth like the great elm

Suffocated and stifled amnesia defined
Removed from what was inclined

Natural in nature always a pull
To breath deep like the bull

Unwind and heal to reset
With one card and one bet

Going for broke leaving a print
One more chance to win this spring

Urge to purge on the verge
Power welling for one last surge

Lasting lies last in line
Im ok I'll be fine

A pile of rocks that seven seal
Laying aim on which is real

Cultures stories turned to dust
By the winner of the lust

Transcending cosmic space and time
Dimensions ripping at my spine

Soothing sounds to block the noise
Back to center where there's poise

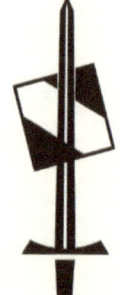

Propelling position purposely sent
Doing my best to make a dent

Seasoned from lifetimes of here and there
With what it takes to truly care

No matter the hardship no matter the pain
Understanding nothings in vain

Concerted effort staying on track
Reaching for light not the black

Watching for trip ups firm on my rug
Sure would be nice for one big hug

Lasting impressions of what should be
Redefining what's meant to be free

Don't fail me now stay strong brave
Time to be everything that you were gave

Another soul awake and alive
After saying goodbye to the hive

Did the work inside out
Through each moment through each doubt

What would come next but a wonderful life
Without the handicap of the matrix strife

Head of the pack leader for sure
She told me love is the cure

Friends forever never thought
Anyone could fill that spot

Fortunate to find such a loving soul
One more plug for one more hole

With this last breath I infuse you with love
When you come back to me above

Close your eyes I'll be there
The children you raise are in my care

They are the warriors for the light
Our connection is very tight

They won't listen to gobbley goo
They have a mission to remove the screw

The doors and windows they will find
Will help humanity be not so blind

My heart is theirs we are ones
The weight they carry is measured in tons

Ever closer ever near
Out of love not of fear

Seranation sings calling out
Triggering greatness what we are about

Inspired to lift through free will
Inner kingdom tuned to chill

Hurry up to wait what's the point
Permission given to anoint

Out of the fog before the fall
Clasping onto a crystal ball

Dream of dreams commencing past
What was never meant to last

Alone in the dark out in the cold
No I won't listen to what I was told

Suffer to see beyond what's real
Getting the wrong end of a bad deal

Vultures prey circling death
As I pray for one more breath

So much darkness each and every
With lead slippers life so heavy

Prison protest shackled and mute
No one in life can give a toot

Past impressions circuits shot
One last chance to share what I got

With each truth comes more pain
Enough to drive a man insane

A heartfelt path ripped in half
Through the tears I try to laugh

Gut check instinct to understand
From what planet did I land

Freed to fire napalm bombs
While I stare into my palms

Pressure mounting overload
Through the mountains on a new road

Not the first or the last
What was once now on blast

Exulting madness to accord
Using blackmail to pull one's cord

Acquiescence to reconcile
Assent abundance to grow the pile

In cahoots to sacrifice
What it means to play nice

Just to clarify what's been done
Religion and god are not as one

Holy scripture used for gain
Harvesting good and bad the same

Accumulation of power and wealth
To the detriment of one's spiritual health

Rain drops falling from the tears
But back in the corner I hear cheers

I'm not innocent oh why's that
Cuz i'm greedy sick and fat

Disregard that last line
While I embellish and write this rhyme

One last life to get shit straight
Amongst the lost I navigate

Holy shit holy hell
What's that stench where's that smell

Flickering candles set a blaze
To burn down what authority says

Rules mandates stupid laws
I don't like women's bras

Catch me living like the free
In the wholeness of totality

Bearing authority of each life
No wonder I never wanted a wife

Nostalgic messages from the grave
Conform the heathen to a slave

Conjured poison mixed and matched
Quite the number on all who've hatched

Lucid dreaming hair on end
No sugar coat won't pretend

To the temple alert the troops
Our enemy is dropping poops

Settle down savage get back in line
Drink it off with a bottle of wine

Detection noted anchor weighed
How far off course we have strayed

Oh my lord take a breath
I have something to confess

I'm not so innocent and not so shy
And sometimes I still get high

I like bitches I like breasts
Someplace for my head to rest

I like satin I like oils
I like showers with the goils

I have lustful thoughts all day
If I had the money I'd just pay

From tips of my toes to the crown of my head
A sense of sickness from the words said

Indignant portrayal wires crossed
Here comes lunch I must toss

Beckoning bonanza turkey stuffed
While the greedy partake in lust

Clinically senile judge and jury
Gobbling down what's a worry

Toothless tyrants barking vile
Out of touch without style

Spring is coming time to clean
Give to self and live the dream

Forged in the fire of dualistic creed
What was once now no need

Carried and guided held by one hand
Without a clue where I might land

Cracking code alert and wise
Breaking bonds untying ties

Quenched in oils tempered and turned
Shadows casted into a lagoon

Laughter's friendship bringing me back
From what was a life so wack

Hocked in love the ultimate sin
There all along how to begin

So damn lonely feeling lost
Trying to figure what was the cost

Losing self to have it all
Off the cliff to free fall

Sequestering strength time and time again
Don't understand why this has been

What a path why this time
So much to clear to embrace this shine

Can't go back can't turn around
Know there's more that hasn't been found

Honest and able to a fault
Something keeps pushing it news says halt

Detached in the moment awake in the now
Not enough words to describe the how

The past is the past so why should I care
You broke my heart and left me standing there

Wasn't who you were wasn't what you meant
Wasn't why I live isn't why I vent

Choices to consider free will of the heart
Brave enough to be honest and let things fall apart

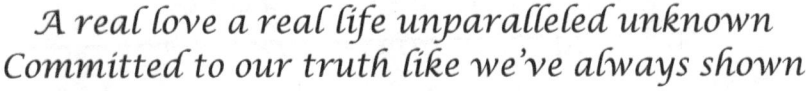

The purpose of the push to hopefully align
Of what was created and placed by devine

A real love a real life unparalleled unknown
Committed to our truth like we've always shown

The swinging door the castle gate
Never closed as the heavens wait

Sustained detachment to bring back
What may cause some heart attack

Breathless breathing body escaped
Seeing a new land and its landscape

Immersed in the glow safe in the sea
Wanting everyone to see what I see

Patterns of old borrowed and bought
Worn out and unsafe now are forgot

Arduous journey riddled by test
What has been said we are the best

Enlightened unencumbered cordage been cut
Floating along out of a rut

Creating division instead of peace
As if been taken mark of the beast

Preparing to rule warlord are sworn
Killing my kind attacked by the swarm

Whatever it takes ruler of rules
As we bow down like we are the fools

Poisoned by power greed in each eye
Bodies lay wasted as mothers cry

Host in some cause blaming our flaws
Seldom a pause into the jaws

Fleasing the pockets dealers get high
Propagating war while innocence dies

Believing the lies of the times
Passed down to us like nursery rhymes

Resurrectionism and powder like dust
Justifying greed and lust

Inundation conform or die
Now a softer version why

Brod net casted invoking rights
Making false claims dimming lights

Tricks and trails writing scripts
High on righteous power trips

Fractured freedom emotions wild
Laying siege to our inner child

Longed to live undivided lives
So it's a time for great strives

Grand deception collecting souls
Prefessing someday levying tolls

Beneath each surface a light so bright
Why control won't give up its fight

Without control no one needs
Fear or shame and where it leads

Torture technique lungs collapsed
Mouth taped shut while evil laughs

Free to believe free to steal
Free to stay on the karmic wheel

Glits and glamor ride portrayed
Built on one man's life they slayed

Christmas season Ho Ho Ho
Burying a truth that I know

Self doubts saddle pressures wave
Wants and needs and what's a crave

Confining constructs opinions galore
Separation rich and poor

Glory given possessions took
As I ponder and have a look

Least the thing that dwells inside
Why we've come to provide

Mysteries magic comes to rest
At a time of the best of the best

Tears of sorrow fade away
Relearning to laugh live love and play

Battered no more by bruising tales
In a history and all its fails

Under the starry skies that fill the night
Comes a reminder we just might

Creations gift pleasure full
Of a blanket made of wool

Escapisms secret internal clock
Releasing anguish unblocking our block

With open mind and wild heart
The voyage begins when we start

Rules written without hold
Nothings free but nothings sold

Pirouetting in the groove
Humble enough and on the move

Without regrets of the rear view mirror
Confident I belong here

Cleansed opinions of a broken heart
That what was given from a tart

Have moved past and moving on
In full strength ample braun

Zealous awe judgment done
Old programming does no longer run

Open to embrace another new start
Past lessons learnt won't tear at this heart

Always an effort to let love shine
In each moment of this sacred shrine

Paradoxical prison of limited beliefs
Built on top of previous beefs

Clear as day with unlimited sight
Organized religion has never been right

Blowing out scripture tooting its horn
Entrapping souls in spiritual porn

Patrons banging head against walls
Removed from nature and her calls

Trapped in bondage with broken wings
Codependent history stings

Growth groomed to stagnate
Better wake up before it's too late

Belligerent stubborn cold to the touch
On life support and one crutch

Fight or flight sink or swim
What's the programming you live in

Coincidence not this vibe
Colonialism destroyed my tribe

Coining subsistence dysfunction in white
In separation high as a kite

Toxic clergy backward views
Branching outward from its pues

Supporting timelines of fractured faith
The scar it's left is all over the place

Take this hand my hummingbird
And leave behind the toxic herd

Grow your wings big and strong
Remove the low vibes that don't belong

Carry your chalic with both hands
From your core true love expands

Dance with destiny flow in tune
What we manifest is coming soon

Delivered from chaos to the heart's content
Our colonies calling from where we were sent

Fixed destination or is it not so
May depend on if we can grow

Out of the old and into the new
With both feet in one shoe

Aiming to live life like a dream
In each moment of each scene

Ever aware tangibles touch
Heroic in nature knowing is such

Mind bending experience secrets revealed
Throughout the process of being healed

Intrepid result gleam in the eyes
Heart full of laughter no compromise

Cosmic awakenings from the skies
Come to us by surprise

Lifting awareness tuning our fork
Head above water we bob like a cork

Full of ambition addressing the now
Fields are planted after the plow

Distressed damsels and man alike
Together we climb on this arduous hike

Inner and outer realms a glow
Lite up the skies revealing the show

One by one then two by two
Immersed in love that creation grew

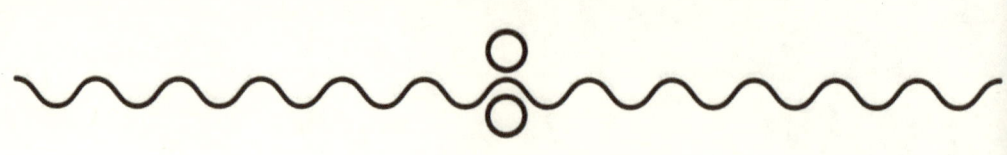

Against the odds amidst the frauds
Manifesting what are gods

Alluring concepts attracting a flock
Temples built on every block

Divisive destruction of free wills goal
Playing games with each soul

Advertising saluations gist
Hands removed at the wrists

Hope revealed in the face of fear
Obligations shadows oh my dear

Picked to point out justifications traps
Written through this form of raps

Sing your song with that sweet voice
Show the people we have a choice

Past begotten when the now is held
In our own power our soul has yelled

Of sovereignties union purpose appears
Washing away the lackluster years

Through sacred eyes connected as one
Conditioned programs no longer run

Brought to the brink entangled in tears
Expunging what was these greatest fears

To this life is this vow
Only the self can show us how

The width of the window determines the view
As to the perceptions that we see through

Lasting impressions that need to be cleared
Life after life of living with fears

Stoic we stand divided we fall
Who is the mastermind behind it all

What sort of criminal tears at our core
Using sick humor to settle the score

Sweet satisfaction comes at a cost
When we get found in the land of the lost

*At long last this search reveals
Those dark shadows are what heals*

*From fractured light to pure bliss
With these lips the universe we kiss*

*As strength from within recreates
A oneness reality permeates*

*Grateful honest trusting this path
Bathing in beauty and a salt bath*

*Toxins removed projections on hold
Intuition is how we know what we're told*

*An elixir of life flowing free
For the brave of a new tree*

Reputation built by the sward
Confiscation of land the reward

Tell me I'm wrong in the name of your god
What can't admit your cult is a fraud

Harvesting innocence collecting fear
Your days are numbered this is clear

Apple eaten to regurgitate
Conformities formula is its fate

Banging one's head against a closed door
Seeking favor in the candy store

True spirits wild witty and wise
Through discernment in the eyes

Arrested to death risen to bleed
Traditions followed by cracked seed

Laugh out loud tearing it up
Breaking the silence spilling this cup

Happy to oblige pleasure to serve
Conformity won't see this curve

The brave and willing will answer the call
Because it's our purpose before the fall

No amount of chaos or space age junk
Will distract us back to the funk

Roll your eyes cross your T's
Your dirty tricks smell like rotten cheese

When these eyes close they only see you
Standing together in the light of the moon

Past and present the futures ours
To take our place amongst the stars

The cosmos calls union devine
As we shift through this earthly grind

Battle with a message of a hearts desire
Out of despair has lit this fire

Propelled to prosper as the universe calls
Back to a home without false walls

So much love to give
So much life to live

So much pending on
So we keep holding strong

So much pain to clear
So we stand in love not fear

So much beauty within
So loneliness can't claim a win

So much potential that we hide
So much distractions that have been tried

So much compassion within our grip
So much confusion what's the trip

The grand illusion of dense and dark
Has set a precedent a sad benchmark

Polluted planet toxic words
3 eyed toads and flightless birds

Rash decisions without foresight
Or is this power ending our fight

Pending prediction opinions oppression
Sick on salvation spreading depression

No I didn't yes I did
Been doing this since I was a kid

Trafficking love through this pen
Tell me do you think that's a sin

Deep in the depth of despairs face
Alone again lost in space

Back bone bent rejection felt
On the heart space was left a welt

Nothing new won't give up
Just one less desire of one less cup

With solid intentions this heart goes out
As love and loyalty replaces doubt

A trust so far not materized
When the sparkle leaves the eyes

To sad to say what could have been
Maybe oneday a special friend

Riding the wind on the wings of hope
In view of a vision through a large scope

Delaying reaction so not to expose
When the inner knowing grows and grows

Realities shifting outside the loop
While power decides just how far it will stoop

Building on influence of rented space
When traditions are threatened to be replaced

Influence peddling of group thought
Ready to fight to keep what they got

Free will finds its way to the truth
When the universe beckons showing vs proof

At attention but not by command
Fighting for goodness in the light band

Instructionally written into DNA
For safe keeping for this day

Intrinsic design in order to learn
When what why how to discern

Amplified vibe to activate
Into the positive that feels so great

Garrison of angels ready to rock
When the clock strikes 12 tickety tock

Sown to see lit to light
Up the universe when we win this fight

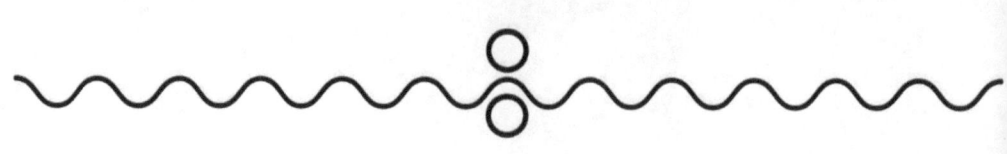

After the haze a path appears
When the conscience has not fears

Undoing the rig to shatter the ceiling
While having fun it's quite appealing

Judge me hate me get in line
Just stay drunk on your wine

Humble pie not tasting so great
This new vibe is like liquid state

Signal fire burning bright
Only love will win this fight

Jealous haters and control freaks
Cleanse your aura of black streaks

How much sorrow can there be
When your loves what set me free

Countless lifetimes in such pain
Starved inside only strain

This debt to you shall be paid
No matter the struggle that must be made

With infinite wisdom of the whole
This love for self will surely grow

Entangled 4-ever our souls rebirth
Playing our part here on earth

Deeply blessed this heart smiles
As it transverses the many miles

Clearing a space for love to move in
Asking the cosmos for a true friend

Calling a match that lies at this core
Most definitely won't be a bore

Strange days in strange ways
Keeping above the dark dense haze

Tempered and vigilant with clear sight
Intuition a glow heart space bright

Remembered to rise and try till no ends
With what matters between two friends

Thanks for the purpose thanks for the chance
4-ever a child in this immaculate dance

Determining matters weighting the scale
Blazing ahead plowing a trail

Why not fight for what's right
Better than being high as a kite

With this last brain cell a torch is lit
What we give is what we get

Rebuking religion and it's cause
Questioning all of its man made laws

Compartmentalizing cause and effect
Coming up with the usual suspect

In an arena with life on the line
A fight to the death before we go blind

No easing up for fear of a slip
Back to the herd and conformities grip

Aimed at ambition in a changing world
While control surges on in what has swirled

Attending agendas borrowed on hope
High on the wealth it uses as dope

Macrosim of the criminal mind
We've never be free because of this kind

Don't need forgiveness don't want a treat
Don't like the limits placed at our feet

Growth is natural growth is great
When power mongers don't affect our fate

Be inspired to leave behind
The things that no longer align

People places material wealth
To improve your emotional health

Take a break or just leave
Give things space and learn to breath

Meditate or medicate free to chose
Only you wear your own shoes

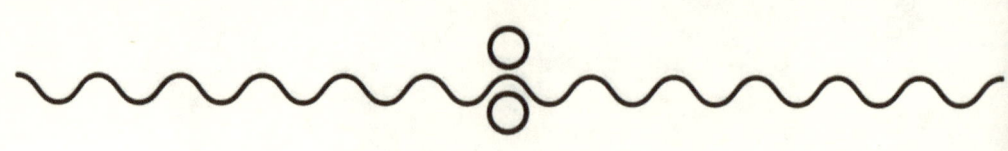

Praised proclamation idolize
Fabric torn in the eyes

Lost in ego detriment
Empty words without content

Costly mistakes tattered dreams
Playing out through money schemes

Varied versions to enslave
Robbing us of what was gave

Shame on authority and its grip
For partaking in this manipulative trip

Sovereignty not salvations
Only way to heal the nations

Intense collision of two souls
Supporting a love that knows no no's

Selected and suited energies locked
To the core they've been rocked

After the suffering through the pain
Two hearts merge on one train

Leaving the station for infinity
Where imagination is our key

Creating beauty in worlds unborn
With the love we've adorn

Tranquility and peace at our fingertips
Connected to source there will be no slips

A once wounded sacred heart
Now is mended to restart

Trauma taken then given back
Set anew on this track

Breaking bonds clearing ground
With this feeling so profound

Absorbing lessons at each turn
Understanding how to discern

An introduction an inner way
Quite mind blowing I must say

Patterned laughter at what's absurd
Of group thought of the herd

Sacred sites sacred soils
Brining tempers to a boil

Dysfunctional relations to same source
We the people the victim of course

Proxy politics preachers puke
Leading the blind without rebuke

Apostates needed to tare down
This fractured way of the clown

Do your research claim your power
Wash this burden in the shower

Clear some space for your own thoughts
Surprise yourself with what you gots

Running scared like rats on a sinking ship
When power sees it's losing its grip

Pointing fingers laying blame
Pleading cases of the insane

Divided factions empires fall
History repeating as we drop the ball

Experiment failing doomed from the start
Death and destruction don't come from the heart

Advisors bought selling lies
Blackmailing opponents while it tries

Out of order court reveals
The monkey slipped on banana peels

Distinct and different where faith fails
Trapped in words and details

Compartments cluttered emotions frayed
To what end the clergy has prayed

Intentions rotting out the core
Collapsing what we must explore

New beginnings don't come easy
And don't happen when the mind is sleazy

Intrepid trails to solidify
Pranks that punk the passerby

Dream a dream let it breath
Keep it safe from the thieve

Done let go in the coma of food
Yes I know this statement is rude

Packing pounds wolfing down
Shocking shaking arteries drown

Processed products flood the shelves
While cows produce hormonal milks

Environments altered chemicals sprayed
To just what is the trade

Forests fall minerals stripped
Evolutions trigger has been tripped

The mothers voice sings in the wind
She'll outlive us in the end

Like a moth to light the heart is drawn
With the body left as a pawn

Chemistries vibe under the skin
Put there from a place within

Depth of being back with kin
When two hearts align again

Highlighting the best in each other
There could never be another

Fortunate free will still exists
So this love can persist

Ditching dogma and traditions held
A story for the ages must be telled

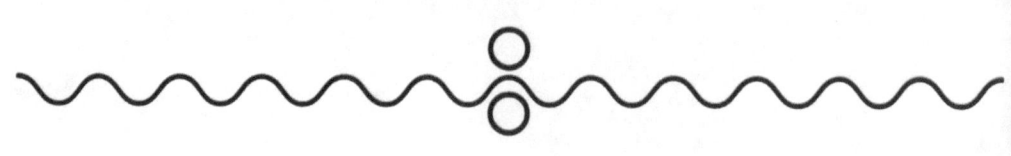

Locked in a love so intense
In the present not past tense

Like a joyous reunion when eyes meet
This love we share is not discrete

Two fish to water in the abyss
Knew it was meant from the very first kiss

Mirrored reflections souls engage
In the mystical dance of a sage

Boundaries crossed borders burned
To find this love that has been earned

You for me, me for you
Magnetic attraction better than glue

Awake and alert above the dirt
Chasing dreams and that skirt

Slashing connections breaking bonds
Adrift on an endless sea of ponds

Lunar illuminations buried deep
Fingers crossed I to shall reap

No compromise will satisfy
If I don't see that look in those eyes

No tease or game will distract
This next soul must make an impact

Hidden to protect guided by grace
The mark is worn with the smile on this face

Too much trauma to transmute
So the voice is put on mute

Can't hold blame when we do our best
Sometimes love finds another nest

Heartstrings stretched to the breaking point
This time there will be no joint

Another lesson of a boundary fail
But this heart won't stay in jail

Adjusted to refine and stay on course
Minor setback not a broken horse

Learn not loss in the cradle of life
This backstab was a quite sharp knife

To what's valued in this space
And the scars that leave a trace

Wasteful greedy disposable
Vengeful angry projected soul

Capital con skating on bills
Feeding the people pharmaceutical pills

Placing trust outside self
While power accumulates more and more wealth

Borrowing bucks kicking the can
Lighting a fire fueled by a fan

Glitching nation out of control
Proud of what it always has stole

Tough transitions not so subtle
When we awake out of trouble

When memories flood in not of this shell
When people keep saying I'm going to hell

When nothing looks normal and some thing seem off
When perceptions change and people scoff

When attributed attitudes lay their claim
When division freeloads stirring the pain

When symbols and signs have view
When what we produce smells like poo

It might be time to rearrange
So this reality doesn't seem so deranged

Whipped to frenzy in a panic state
As old methods still create

Castles crumble under the boot
While patriots give their final salute

In decadence walls collapse
When the people see the traps

Battle tested the sovereign sing
The blind won't see what we bring

Long the list that grows ripe
Above confusion and useless gripe

Independent but as one
The war we wage is almost won

Hand held out to hold that heart
The final piece of the missing part

Don't know how don't know why
When your near I seem to cry

Overwhelmed the intensity grows
Shivering tingles to these toes

This life has been no smooth ride
From love is where I've tried to hide

Tripped up out of the blue
Recovering the best I know how to

Back to the blueprint to tweak the ink
One of these times neither will blink

Known to some but not most
What it's like to be a ghost

Altered reality energies shift
On the clouds is where we drift

Dreaming dreams supporting the whole
Good vibrations to the soul

Jotting down notes inventory taken
No this life has not been forsaken

Bathed in salt tuner tuned
No more living like a baboon

Higher and higher awareness grows
Through the light this love flows

Exercised in mystery strengthened by blessings
Living to learn whatever lessons

Limits and labels pushed aside
In the trash they reside

Trippin on love the magical brain
Doing the maintenance to maintain

High as fuck crazy indeed
Can you believe I don't read

Lifelong journey to complete
No competition can compete

Watery grave for powers run
What comes next will be fun

How many directions can there be
Which agenda will set us free

What intentions are our friends
Who's there for us in the end

Why the deception in the now
Where is the manuel to show us how

What once was great now so sad
Soul sucking criminals have made us mad

Influence casting shadows dark
Dull and dreary without spark

Peace not war love not hate
Doesn't that sound like something great

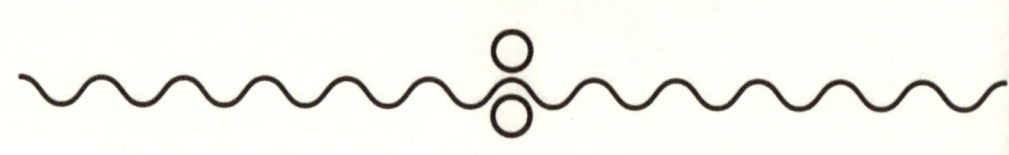

Only truth will set us free
Out of the grip of conformity

Only the purpose of unconditional love
Can heal our hearts so here's a shove

Back to basics friction relieved
Clearing space for trust not believed

In the now not past tense
Spirit lifted from the dense

Glory given to life itself
And the natural beauty that rewards health

Monsters of madness shall have no sway
When love is learned in every way

Built to bury the fakes and lies
Day after day this soul tries

Exposed to blinding emerald glow
Expressing love that we must grow

Demi god leaders and powers trolls
Grab your shovels and dig your holes

The people shall rise and claim what's right
With our connection we hold tight

Treaties and oaths we refuse
To keep being so abused

Capitalist communists socialist a like
Pack your bags and take a hike

My fallen angel with broken wings
I sense your light through all other things

That beating heart goes pitter patter
And is the key to climb life's ladder

With soul growth grown and intact
The burden you carried is off your back

Chose wise my friend and stay alert
You hold the power to avert

Stay close to your child that is within
Adjust your posture with that shy grin

Remember from where we have come
Experience life as not to be numb

Anticipation yearning burning desire
Match is lit to lite the fire

Eternal flame with endless fuel
Decadence meets its final duel

Clairvoyant candy gumballs galore
With wisdoms wings to explore

Among us travelers from other realms
As timelines converge when the bell sounds

An amazing mixture of talisman
Here for freedom to claim the win

Ending the reign of tyrannies face
In just one blink it will be erased

Eyes wide open seeing what's up
Letting loves elixir spill from this cup

Hasn't been easy sometimes not smooth
But life is better when love is the groove

Those cherished moments when hearts melt
Something so deep sensation is felt

Heightened awareness of just how great
When love becomes a permanent state

With ego aside new focus defines
What lives in the heart giving us signs

Thank you so much cherished one
Who knew life could be so fun

Granted freedom at this birth
To move freely upon this earth

Infused with a soul that will never die
Here to grow learn and try

Out from the shadows basking in tune
Manifesting what comes soon

Free from hast settling in
Finding the strength from within

Pissing off parrot talking points
Watching discomfort fill the joints

Lasting impressions most certainly expose
What wisdom grows and ignorance knows

Old guard method to perpetuate
Division and chaos and its hate

Factions pitted weapons at the ready
On a diet it must feed steady

Simple solution that won't pay bills
The thought of peace gives power chills

Conflict conditioned artillery aimed
What seems normal can't be sustained

Snake around the old goats neck
Who writes history writes the check

Played out posture the killing stops
When the pine runs out for each box

Hiding to hold this vision of light
Asking for one moment to be right

Calling new in calling old out
Shifting and blending ignoring tout

Seditious rumors gossip at best
There might be something to get off this chest

Limiting views loyalty lies
The many ways power tries

So many secrets sealed lips
Power stays high as it trips

Serious problem serious solution
Stopping toxic and its pollution

Seeking the solace of salvations seed
What sort of garden grows this sort of weed

Broken panes in each door
Counting backwards to keep score

Clicky clergy one of none
Judging zealots commandment done

Slate to clear canvas clean
To erase what's been obscene

Gariatric procession of sold souls
Whos intentions have had tolls

Guarded goons in false robes
Take a lick from the poisonous toads

*Trained to reach deep inside
To reveal secrets we hide*

*Sometimes painful sometimes sweet
Sometimes change is not so discreet*

*Sometimes words don't describe
When with soul family in the vibe*

*Sometimes we might be misled
As opinions twirl around our head*

*Sometimes barrier stand in our way
That we've imagined might wreck our day*

*Sometimes life seems but a dream
Like a gentle flowing stream*

Mixed up words mangled myths
Main stream mouths and their twists

Attention captured distractions glued
No wonder people are so screwed

Harvesting anguish fears delight
Conditions ripe for some plight

Calculated cosmic dressing room
Still acting like the first baboon

The sly snake slithers in tall grass
Planting its fangs into your ass

So honor the sun as she recedes
And find yourself some better reads

To miseries chagrin the wounded soul
Comes a message we all should know

Better to have loved than just lived
Who we are is what we give

Influenced instincts characterize
True perception who's in the eyes

No amount of bubble wrap
Can keep us safe from conformities crap

Brazen attempt to hold sway
And claim for itself the only way

On the outside looking in
There will be no more of miseries chagrin

Particles charged sanctum sealed
Harvest coming for the yield

Synchronicities signs awareness grown
Content on a path newly shown

Remembrance of just how greatness is born
When we've cleared what caused scorn

Energy signature lifted in vibe
Not what we're usto out of contrive

Natural transition back to the child
Lucid and freeing can be wild

Holding one's breath for the next test
Looking forward to a nice long rest

Sense of direction steered off course
Plotting and scheming questing source

Trust is within not outside
The history we've learned is gunna collide

With those awake and aware of our role
To reconcile authorities toll

Uncomfortable hardships of burdens imposed
Shall be the end of what authority sows

Click bait propaganda of AI tools
Leading the way for ignorant fools

One more layer to squeeze and confine
The energy we were given from the divine

Increased intensity forced to face
The deep dark shadows of the human race

Tears will be shed connections broke
The many lies will become a joke

Solid ground will evaporate
As new eyes focus on what we wait

Clandestine calling to fill the void
To detach from what's annoyed

While corruption wages war again
We hold steady with our kin

We've seen the plot we know our place
When this is over there will be no trace

Circumstances set harvest is ripe
Complaining is over so don't gripe

The winning team has learned how to learn
Through awareness we discern

Our inner guidance feeds our soul
Our loyal commitment is how we grow

Crafted to create our own path
In the sea we take our bath

Hard wire connection to our gifts
Like sand on a beach reality shifts

Find what was given be present stay clear
Stand in your power never in fear

Adverse to compassion and collective thought
Asking the questions to get where we got

Writing riddles to break free
Looking for my family

As if this race has no clue
Trapped in anguish feeling blue

Ripped from the womb left to die
Now with wings free to fly

Permissions given greenlight to go
Ever expanding willing to grow

Calm and convinced solutions exist
So the search goes on as I persist

Hold this heart next to yours
Allow true love to produce cures

Eons aching drenched in pain
I your Tarzan you my Jane

Moonlight through the mist whispers try
To heal ones heart that has gone dry

Foggy amnesia that once blurred sight
In reconnection and feeling tight

Falling leaves under an autumn moon
A reminder winter is coming soon

Changing the guard to coincide
When frigid air keeps us inside

By a warm bright fire and homemade soup
Close bonds rejoice in a cozy coop

Preparation in order to make it through
In the comfort we find in the love we grew

Change is no accident and good for the soul
Like winters chicken soup in your bowl

It's good to slow down as to reflect
And remember what's dear and what we protect

Why bother trying in the face of denial
Ignorance has no genuine smile

Just another mask to hide the sorrow
Thats repeated every tomorrow

Confounding condition imprinted design
Capturing what it can not define

Blueprint madness hidden from sight
Behind the vale built on fright

Spiritual degenerates trapped in vile
Projecting its sickness in the same old style

Got your monkey here's your wrench
Coming soon to clear that stench

Persistently passed prescribed and described
Stealing innocence robbing high vibe

Denial dances in many a shades
Always as truth seems to evade

Mockery muse buying the ruse
Leaving clues spiritual blues

Do as your told because its written
Or a life without will be smitten

One joke after another
What's to say ooooh brother

New in century classic in herd
Pilgrims buying every word

Holding the secrets that we tell
So our soul don't end up in hell

Penance paid hail mary
OMG that sounds scary

Next a list of blackmail deeds
Conquering stealing how it feeds

Wretched betrayal indignant tone
Fat been eaten off every bone

Wicked kingdom burns inside
Because it knows it can not hide

Wholly mother son of sam
Some see through your dirty scam

Pleased to meet this humming place
Alone in nature in this grace

Gentle breeze blows flowers in bloom
Completely detached from the legions of doom

On the outside looking in
Communing with nature free of sin

Open to receive conditioned to shine
Expecting a role within the divine

Quietly sitting in the stream of life
In this state she becomes a wife

Grateful to find what stayed hidden
Giving new meaning to what is forbidden

*That flickering spark that's still there
Is why this heart is willing to dare*

*Life can bring gifts in the dark
That can reignite that inner spark*

*Life can throw water in our face
To wake us up and remember grace*

*Life can put sand in our jar
When separation gets to far*

*Life can hold meaning quite profound
When we tune to silent sound*

*Treasures await the bold and brave
A chance to discover what we was gave*

Astounding recognition of just how great
Being in hi vibe is the permanent state

No one gets in without permission
Nothing can stop this soul mission

Lifted and lite luggage lost
Yes true freedom has a cost

Not for the average whiny bitch
Moving forward without a hitch

Past transgressions not the style
When value lives in why we smile

Horses hitched to burdens cross
Have had their toll and a cost

*To whom who wear a mask to hide
From the fear they keep inside*

*Or the guilt from shames disgrace
From not fitting in at this place*

*It's our oneness authority fears
Cuz we stand out amongst our peers*

*Power knows its lost touch
We aren't the eggs from its clutch*

*Were not its prey we won't be bought
And no blackmail will take what we got*

*Rest assured the wait will reveal
When full disclosure has sealed the deal*

With or without black or white
No one can stop the coming light

Brilliant in design free from flaws
The universe has her own laws

So if she call you it's time to partake
And assist the lifted in driving a stake

Though the heart of what criminals do
There will be no prisoners when we get through

Corruption has reigned for long enough
Enslaving the people making it tough

The run is over fate been sealed
Celebration is gifted to the healed

Give me a chance to introduce myself
I'm not your average beat down elf

My angel wings were singed in a fire
My passions in life were consumed by desire

My focus in life was seduction and lust
But what was never lost was trust

Through honesties window a fresh breath of air
Willing to take the ultimate dare

Clearing trauma whatever it takes
Have quite the knack for uncovering fakes

My goal is simple to never forget
What I've been through the crazy shit

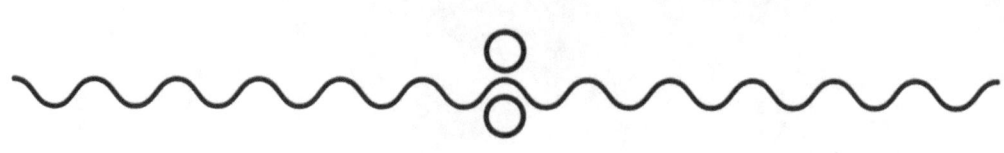

Sitting here thinking about the lives we touch
And the influence we have to little too much

How acts of kindness are felt and received
How through each lenz we each perceive

How what sort of person could be so cold
How others can bring it being bold

How what we keep hidden keeps us trapped
How each of us has inspiration to tap

How the many a paths that lie and wait
How with the brave we resonate

How at the end of the day we each have a plan
Its whats in our hearts that I'm a fan

What gaps we close to unite
Are signs of growth and feeling right

One to another false egos dead
With true action not words we've said

Sparks to embers, embers to fire
As passion fills hearts with desire

Landscape littered with horse drawn carts
With broken axles and no spare parts

Old abandoned nature reclaims
Covering tracks on the plains

Spirit the witness as the waves invade
Into a land where our ancestors laid

Brother of mine friend for life
I know you miss your beautiful wife

Your children are here still safe and sound
It's in their hearts she will be found

My vibe goes out to heal your hurt
I know you'd give a stranger your shirt

The stages of grief are never nice
So keep your head above the frozen ice

I'm right here for you my big bro
I hope from this your soul will grow

At last a laugh as dimensions shift
When truth lays claim to lies that grift

Emotional coordinates cycling back
Splitting hairs white and black

Synchronistic awareness grows
In the ebbs and the flows

Crashing through boundaries full steam ahead
Collecting wisdom the ethers shed

Darwin deniers your shorts are full
Of the waste of the bull

Feeling fantastic in this radiant vibe
Lifting awareness in the eternal tribe

You're a ray of light in the dark night sky
In your presence I often cry

Our bond is tight you've lead me home
The love you gave the love you've shown

No distraction can come between
This connection that can't be seen

Incognito this light stays bright
Where it's hidden out of sight

Gentle at times sturdy and strong
Sweet sounds sining brand new songs

Whatever the risk whatever the lesson
I'll be the salad you are the dressn

Standing in silence listening close
Blending in like a ghost

Ticket punched enjoying the ride
Still alive after three times died

So much to say so few words
Pigs and pearls butts and turds

Killing me smalls sandlot full
On which leg must love pull

No discounts or coupon book
Will stop the criminal or the crook

Headstrong egos do detest
Whatever the title not impressed

Out of the pack off the track
Back to the wild to find that child

Lost then found on sacred ground
Position spotted destination plotted

Trivial nonsense left in a cave
Venturing forward being brave

Flexible perception mirrors gone
No poster child or court pawn

Restricted access the doorbell rings
As treasure flows from all things

Through dark shadows fractures entice
Paths in life that aren't so nice

As if ignorance has no mirror
What to some seems quite clear

Collection of feathers from the do-do-bird
Deft dumb and blind in the herd

Cease and desist outline described
Power the culprit blackmail the bribe

Monsters of mayhem executing justice
Say to the people you must trust us

Horrified council waits at the ready
Fact or fiction is there a yeti

Approaching each day with what matters
Not into climbing corporate ladders

Have no intention of owning the land
It's not for sale from where I stand

Rebellious by nature free like a bird
Most days are good some are absurd

With an understanding that sees in the dark
To where was laid our first spark

Traveling dimensions not seen to the eyes
Feeling fulfilled contentment defies

Irrational illogic say it ain't so
What in the world how could I know

In these thoughts are herd the call of the wild
Speaking to that inner child

Where freedom and health are put first
To try and quench that endless thirst

Never fit in no longer try
Not gonna live a life of a lie

Entrusted to carry a bucket of gold
That only has value if it is sold

Sensing a cycle surging ahead
Clowning the criminals I see as dead

Among us they walk before us they fall
The cannon is ready to fire its ball

What of corruptions body of pain
Influencing a world gone insane

Silently suffering intrusions infusion
To what power targets in its abusin

Stagnate and stifle covertly through fear
Obeying the words we often hear

Whip in hand brand in other
As the free run for cover

Sick and twisted false throne glory
Narrative neutered in its story

Hay loft empty dead crop on the vine
Guess this year there will be no wine

A life worth living is the one we must find
Not the one of the daily grind

Freedoms our friend control our foe
What we receive is what we shall sow

Pins in a cushion tricks of the trade
It doesn't make sense for what has been prayed

True inspiration comes from within
Not from the pages of dead men sin

Tasteless meals countless lies
As the human spirit dies

To: Why we are

That which was hidden now been revealed
Mind body soul has been healed

Something was missing didn't know what
One in a million door opened then shut

Closed off from fatalities dogmas deeds
Clearing space for new seeds

Rules of engagement redefined
The reason power has left us blind

Secret weapon primed to tase
When this experiment has a new phase

Tribal war paint under the flesh
Soul of a warrior with each breath

www.ingramcontent.com/pod-product-compliance
Lightning Source LLC
LaVergne TN
LVHW091534070526
838199LV00001B/56